Greater Th

Montenegro

50 Travel Tips from a Local

Redina Zela

Order Information: To order this title please email lbrenenc@gmail.com or visit GreaterThanATourist.com. A bulk discount can be provided.

Cover Template Creator: Lisa Rusczyk Ed. D. using Canva.
Cover Creator: Lisa Rusczyk Ed. D.
Image: https://pixabay.com/en/booked-montenegro-kotor-balkan-995041/

Lock Haven, PA

ISBN: 9781549881916

>TOURIST

Redina Zela

BOOK DESCRIPTION

Are you excited about planning your next trip?

Do you want to try something new?

Would you like some guidance from a local?

If you answered yes to any of these questions, then this Greater Than a Tourist book is for you.

Greater than a tourist by Redina Zela offers the inside scoop on Montenegro. Most travel books tell you how to sightsee. Although there's nothing wrong with that, as a part of the Greater than a Tourist series, this book will give you tips from someone who lives at your next travel destination. In these pages, you'll discover local advice that will help you throughout your trip.

Travel like a local. Slow down and get to know the people and the culture of a place. By the time you finish this book, you will be eager and prepared to travel to your next destination.

Redina Zela

TABLE OF CONTENTS

Redina Zela

Our Story

Notes

DEDICATION

This book is dedicated to anyone visit Montenegro. This is a simple guide with the top reasons why to visit this country. It's suitable for all ages so don't hesitate to get your copy.

ABOUT THE AUTHOR

Redina is a girl currently living in Tirana, Albania. She's finishing her studies in Tirana City. One of her hobbies is traveling and she has decided to visit all European countries at least once. Montenegro is near her hometown so she has had the chance to visited often. Redina likes to spend her vacations there but every time in a different city. Hope you enjoy her traveling guide!

HOW TO USE THIS BOOK

The Greater Than a Tourist book series was written by someone who has lived in an area for over three months. The goal of this book is to help travelers either dream or experience different locations by providing opinions from a local. The author has made suggestions based on their own experiences. Please do your own research before traveling to the area in case the suggested places are unavailable.

FROM THE PUBLISHER

Traveling can be one of the most important parts of a person's life. The anticipation and memories that you have are some of the best. As a publisher of the Greater Than a Tourist book series, as well as the popular 50 Things to Know book series, we strive to help you learn about new places, spark your imagination, and inspire you. Wherever you are and whatever you do I wish you safe, fun, and inspiring travel.

Lisa Rusczyk Ed. D.

CZYK Publishing

WELCOME TO > TOURIST

INTRODUCTION

Montenegro (meaning "Black Mountain" in Montenegrin) is a country located in Southeastern Europe. It has a coast on the Adriatic Sea to the south-west and is bordered by Croatia to the west, Bosnia and Herzegovina to the northwest, Serbia to the northeast, and Albania to the southeast. Its capital and largest city is Podgorica, while Cetinje is designated as the Prijestonica (Пријестоница), meaning the former Royal Capital City.

Montenegro is a member of the United Nations, the Organization for Security and Co-operation in Europe, CEFTA, Council of Europe and Montenegro is also a founding member of the Union for the Mediterranean. It is also an official candidate for membership in the European Union and NATO.

1. Getting There

Montenegro has two main airports. The first one is located in the capital, Podgorica, and the second one is in Tivat, which is a city near Kotor.

If your country is located near Montenegro you can always choose to come with a bus. A bus would be fun if you're traveling with a group of friends.

If you own a GPS you can travel with your own car because the road is good enough so you won't have a hard time driving.

Your way of transport depends where you want to go so remember to check the map first.

2. Accommodation

The accommodation scene in Montenegro can be somewhat frustrating. Partly due to the country's premature marketing as a "luxury" destination, **hotels** are almost uniformly overpriced – in some areas, it can be tough to find anything for under €50 in peak season. A few **hostels** have opened up in recent years, though competition is yet to hone quality.

Many travellers end up staying in **private rooms**. Prices vary dramatically depending on the quality of room, the time of year and the location in question – rates in less heralded towns dip below €10 per person in off-season, though you may pay three times more during summer in popular destinations such as Budva and Kotor. In warmer months, proprietors with rooms to spare wait for travellers outside the bus stations – see what's on offer before handing over any cash – while travel agencies are often able to make bookings.

3. Getting Around

For a country with such a small population, the frequency of intercity **buses** is quite remarkable. In addition, Montenegro has poured substantial funds into the upgrading of its main travel arteries, and travel times are accordingly short. A **train** line heads to Bar from the Serbian border – a beautiful journey.

While services are infrequent, prices are dirt-cheap and almost every inch of track affords breathtaking views, especially the run into Podgorica from the Serbian border – be sure to sit on the western side of the train.

4. Travel Essentials

BUSINESS HOURS

Offices are open weekdays from 8 to 4. Shops are generally open weekdays from 9 to 9, Saturday from 8 to 1, though some shut for lunch around 2 and may close for as long as three hours. Large supermarkets will have longer working hours and won't close for lunch. Banks stay open weekdays from 9 to 6, Saturday from 9 to 1.

CURRENCY

The official currency has been the euro since 2002, despite the fact that Montenegro has not yet entered the European Union; negotiations are under way for its EU membership.

5. Food And Drink

Montenegro's **restaurant** scene is a little disappointing. In tourist areas, traditional meals have largely been pushed out by pizza and pasta, and prices have risen beyond those of neighbouring countries. Traditional restaurants are known as *konoba*, and can help those willing and able to escape said Italian staples.

Menu items to look out for include grilled kebabs (*ćevapčići*), cabbage leaves stuffed with mincemeat (*sarma*), bean soup with flecks of meat (*pasulj*), goulash (*gulaš*), and the artery-clogging *karađorđe vasnicla*, a breaded veal cutlet roll stuffed with cheese.

Vegetarians can take refuge in the hearty salads available almost everywhere. Also ubiquitous are the Turkish snack staples of *burek*, pastry filled with meat, cheese, spinach and occasionally mushroom, and syrupy baklava sweets.

Coffee (*kafa*) is consumed with almost religious fervour, usually served Turkish-style with unfiltered grounds, but also available espresso-style. Strong-as-hell **rakija** remains the alcoholic drink of choice – you'll be offered it constantly if visiting someone's home – but travellers usually subsist on some fine local beers, most notably Nikšićko, which also comes in an excellent dark variety (*tamno*). There are good **wines** too, with Vranac an interesting local grape variety – the Plantaže label has it in their roster, and is both cheap and easy to find.

6. Starting With The Capital

The capital of Montenegro is Podgorica. What you can do here? This is exactly what we're going to talk about in the next chapters.

We're going to start with Saborni Hram Hristovog Vaskrsenja. In English it's translated Cathedral of the Resurrection of Christ.

History

Construction of the church of around 14,000 square feet began in 1993 to a design by Predrag Ristić. Consecration occurred on October 7, 2014 on the occasion of the 1700-year anniversary of the Edict of Milan on freedom of religion.

Architecture

The Orthodox Arts Journal writes that the cathedral is "certainly one of the most interesting Orthodox churches built in our times. Unlike other new cathedrals we have seen recently, the exterior does not seek to reflect High-Byzantine perfection. Rather, it is a charmingly eccentric design. It has the slightly awkward qualities of any real cathedral, expressing the cultural tensions between the high Imperial style and the capabilities of local craftsmen." The church, with its twin towers and prominent arch is clearly influenced by the medieval Cathedral of St. Tryphon in Kotor, with Romanesque, Italianate, and Byzantine influences.

The interior is heavily adorned with iconographic murals with gold backgrounds, marble floors and furnishings

7. Moraca River Canyon

The road running within the Moraca River Canyon is one of the most spectacular roads in the world. Located in Montenegro, the road traversing the canyon is called E65. Riddled with countless cliff-side bends and tunnels, this road is basically out to get you, but if you survive you'll be blown away by the beauty of the landscape that surrounds you.

Moraca River Canyon separates Moračke planine range from Sinjajevina range. It's located between Podgorica and Kolasin. This part of the canyon is called "Platije". The highway is built along the edge of the narrow canyon.

Moraca canyon covers the south-eastern part of the central region of Montenegro. This road is passable during most part of the year. It is closed only in case of abundant snowing or great rockslides. The main travel route connecting the north and the south of Montenegro runs along the Moraca Canyon.

The surface of the road is asphalted. It includes several tunnels and is very dangerous. This road is passable during most part of the year. It is closed only in case of abundant snowing or great rockslides.

The road is in dreadful condition and requires strong nerves to negotiate it. Any barriers along the edge afford little more than token protection. Thus, you can enjoy in observing the beautiful contrast between steep, dark cliffs and light, green river, while round, white peaks of Bjelasica glow in the distance, at moments, this beauty becomes scary!

8. Vladimir Vysotsky Monument

Vladimir Vysotsky monument in Podgorica. Vladimir Semyonovich Vysotsky (1938-1980) was Russian singer, songwriter, poet and actor. On monument is written:

mne: ...ja zalim u ovom zivotu sto nemam korijena dva, sto drugom domovinom mojom ne zovem Crnu Goru ja!

English: ...I regret in this life that I don't have two roots, and as my second homeland I can't name Montenegro.

9. Waterfall Niagara

Did you know that Montenegro has a Niagara Waterfall?

These edges Montenegro are renowned for their fantastic beauty where Tsievna mountain river flows among the hills, taking its origin on the border with Albania. Getting on the territory of the former Yugoslavia, the river continues its way already in mountainous terrain, which gradually turns into the plain with a large number of fields.

There is, at the junction where Tsievna meets the river Moraca and is a beautiful waterfall Niagara. We can say, in the area of Niagara beautiful nature artificially created by man, including the waterfall itself.

The fact that the local authorities have decided to create a kind of a small reservoir, neobohimoe for watering the vast number of fields. The resulting lake, located on a hill flows down from the height of a ten, recalling a miniature waterfall.

10. Millennium Bridge

The **Millennium Bridge** is a cable-stayed bridge that spans the Morača River, in Podgorica, Montenegro.

It was built by the Slovenian company *Primorje*, and opened on July 13, 2005, Montenegro's National Day. It quickly became one of the city's most prominent landmarks.

The bridge is 173 metres long, and the pylon soars 57 m above the roadbed. Twelve cables support the roadway deck, while twenty-four more are attached to the counterweights, creating an imposing image.

The roadway carries two lanes of traffic and a pedestrian walkway in each direction. The bridge connects the *Boulevard of Ivan Crnojević* in the city centre and *July 13 street* in the new part of city, thus relieving the other congested bridges connecting the city center with the densely populated districts over the Morača river.

"Little Montenegro! He Lifted up the words and nodded at them- with his smile. The smile comprehended Montenegro's troubled history and sympathized with the brave struggles of the Montenegrin people. It appreciated fully the chain of national circumstances, which had elicited this tribute from Montenegro's warm little heart."

- *F Scott. Fitzgerald*

11. Plantaze Winery

One of the best things to do in Podgorica is – you guessed it, drinking!

A little-known fact about Podgorica is that it's home to the largest unbroken vineyard in Europe, owned by Plantaze Winery. Whenever you go to a restaurant in Montenegro, you'll find Plantaze wine and you can pick up a bottle in supermarkets for as little as €2.

You can visit Plantaze's Sipcanik wine cellar and do wine tastings. There are two options:

- Three wines and Njeguski cheese are €10 per person.
- Five wines and gourmet canapes are €30 per person.

All tastings include a ride through the vineyard on a tourist train, a guided tour of Sipcanik wine cellar and an expert guide through your tasting. They also have horse-riding experiences for €30 per hour… best do that *before* your tasting!

Interestingly, the wine cellar used to be a secret

underground aircraft hangar. It was bombed in 1999 and abandoned until it found a second lease on life as a wine cellar. It now houses around two million litres of wine!

12. Horse Riding

Just 15 minutes from Podgorica, you'll find Mountain Riders Ranch in the heart of the Komani Highlands.

Mountain Riders have horse treks for everyone, from complete beginners to experienced riders. Exploring the country on horseback is a fun and exciting way to explore true off-the-tourist-track destinations in Montenegro. You'll see remote villages, pick fruit in the orchards of abandoned stone villages and have riverside picnics.

13. Podgorica Museum

Most of Montenegro's historical artefacts are kept on display in the old royal capital, Cetinje. But some of them have been kept in Podgorica and you'll find an interesting display of items from everyday life in this region.

The most interesting display here is the antiquities from Doclea, the old Roman town just north of Podgorica. There are also archaeological, ethnographic, historical and cultural-historical displays.

14. Stara Varos - Old Town

Not so much and old town like the ones in Kotor, Budva and Herceg Novi, Podgorica's old town was built under Ottoman rule and it's an old shopping district with winding streets full of jewellery shops, restaurants and boutiques.

Podgorica was heavily bombed during WWII so not much of it remains. The only remnants of Turkish are two mosques and a clock tower. The clock tower was rebuilt in 2005 – look out for signs for Sahat Kula.

15. Nightlife

In a city of 200,000 where the locals love to party, there's always something going on. The best place to go is Bokeska and adjacent Njegoseva streets in downtown Podgorica. There are lots of cafes and bars and it's busy most nights.

For nightclubs where you can dance until the early hours, head over the football stadium where you'll find District and Gavroche (Ulica 19 December, Podgorica). District is a nightclub and Gavroche is a culture centre which often hosts indie bands and concerts.

This was the last chapter about the capital, Podgorica. In the next ones we're going to talk about other beautiful towns.

16. Budva

Budva is a Montenegrin town on the Adriatic Sea, former bishopric and present Latin Catholic titular see. It has around 14,000 inhabitants, and it is the centre of Budva Municipality. The coastal area around Budva, called the Budva riviera, is the center of Montenegrin tourism, known for its well-preserved medieval walled city, sandy beaches and diverse nightlife. Budva is 2,500 years old, which makes it one of the oldest settlements on the Adriatic coast.

Budva is home to the Adriatic Fair (Jadranski sajam), the only specialized exhibition venue in Montenegro. It hosts numerous trade fairs throughout the year, including the only auto show in Montenegro, held annually in autumn.

Gambling tourism is also popular in Budva, as many hotels have attached casinos. Maestral hotel and casino in Pržno are particularly popular among international gamblers, but other large hotels have also attracted players from European countries. The 2006 James Bond film *Casino Royale* is partly set in the eponymous casino in the fictional Montenegrin Hotel Splendide, thus giving a boost to Budva's profile as a gambling destination.

17. Citadela

The Budva Citadel is ancient and beautiful, and set at the highest point of the town itself. Thought to have been built atop the Budva ancient Acropolis, the views from within the citadel are unequalled, showcasing the tremendous splendour of one of Montenegro's most celebrated locations.

The Citadel was built in 1936 by the Austrian Army, in order to house the hoards of troops that were stationed at the coast during WW2, and is not only a tourist attraction due to its privileged viewpoint. It is also the location of the town museum, and a stately library, which are both open to the public.

In the evening, the Citadel and surrounding area comes alive with bars and restaurants. In the summer months, it is transformed into a stage for the annual City Theatre Festival. At any time of year or day, the Citadel is enchanting and historic, gently unfurling Budva's past, or playing a part in its present.

18. Sveti Nikola

Sveti Nikola island is located opposite to the town of Budva, 1 kilometre (0.6 miles) from Budva's old town. The island is 2 kilometres (1 mile) long, and it has an area of 36 hectares (89 acres). The highest point on the island is a cliff that rises 121 metres (397 feet) above the sea.

The island is a popular excursion site in the Budva area. It has three bigger sandy beaches with a total length of 840 metres (2,760 feet), and numerous small beaches around the island, accessible only by boat.

Deer inhabit the uncultivated part of the island. The island is called *Školj* by locals, which comes from the word "Školjka" which means shell, because of its shape, while the youth refer to it as "Hawaii" island.

19. Sveti Stefan

Sveti Stefan is a small islet and 5-star hotel resort on the Adriatic coast of Montenegro, approximately 6 kilometres (3.7 mi) southeast of Budva.

The resort, known commercially as **Aman Sveti Stefan**, includes part of the mainland, where the **Villa Miločer**(Montenegrin: [vîla mîlɔ̞t̪ʃe̞r̩]) part of the resort is located. An Adriatic playground for the rich and famous from the 1960s to the 1980s, the hotel is now a 5-star franchise hotel of the international group of Aman Resorts, completed in 2009 and operating under a 30-year lease. Formerly an island, Sveti Stefan is now connected to the mainland by a narrow isthmus. The resort in total contains 50 rooms, cottages and suites on the island and 8 grand suites at the Villa Miločer.

20. Podmaine Monastery

Podmaine Monastery is a Serbian Orthodox monastery built in the 15th century by the Crnojević noble family in Podmaine near Budva, Zeta (modern day Montenegro). The monastery has two churches.

The exact year of establishment of the monastery is unknown. The church of Dormition of the Mother of God was built in the 15th century and reconstructed in 1630 while its larger church (Church of St. Petka) was built in 1747.

Metropolitan Danilo I Petrović-Njegoš died in Podmaine Monastery in 1735. He was buried in the monastery but his remnants were later moved to Cetinje. Dositej Obradović lived several months in this monastery when he visited Boka in 1764.

In 1830 Petar II Petrović-Njegoš, based on the request of the emperor of Russia, sold Podmaine Monastery and

Stanjevići Monastery together with their estates to the Austrian Empire.

Njegoš wrote parts of his masterpiece The Mountain Wreath in Podmaine Monastery.

Sometimes in the waves of change we find our true direction.

- Unknown

21. International Carnival In Budva

The Riviera of Budva is known for its festivals, carnivals, and fishermen gatherings. It is a great experience to visit Budva during some of those events.

The international carnival, so-called “Spring Night under Masks”, will take place in the metropolis of tourism from 02th to 04thof May. Budva becomes a city of masks! It gathers a large number of visitors from the region.

First day of Carnival is dedicated to Abrum (public call to participation in Carnival) and thematic evenings organized in cafés in the Old Town. A large carnival parade will be held on the second day of Carnival and will be followed by entertainment program and concerts of music stars, A-capella vocal groups and DJs performances at several squares inside and outside the Old Town. Carnival groups from 12 countries with over 2,500 participants join the local carnival group “Feštađuni” in the Large International Parade.

A small carnival parade and as well as rich cultural-entertainment program for children, with over 1,100 children from five countries, will be organized on the last day of Carnival.

The organizers of this event are Tourism Organization of Budva, Municipality of Budva and NGO "Feštadjuni".

22. Jaz Beach

Jaz (Serbian Cyrillic: Јаз, pronounced [jâːz]) is a beach in the Budva Municipality in Montenegro. It is located 2.5 km west of Budva. It consists of two parts, one 850 m long and the other, formerly a nudist beach, 450 m long. It is a pebble beach, with a campground along the greater part of the beach (capacity 2,000 lots).

While it is a popular beach for sunbathing and camping, and is one of the longer beaches in Montenegro, it has gained international prominence as a host of numerous concerts and happenings in recent years.

The vast hinterlands of the Jaz beach are considered among the greatest potentials for tourism development on the Montenegrin coast, as there are few undeveloped areas left on the coast besides Jaz (notably Buljarica, Velika Plaža and Ada Bojana).

The Rolling Stones played a show on July 9, 2007, as a

part of their A Bigger Bang Tour. For the performance, a large field in the beach hinterland was leveled, fenced, and made accessible by refurbishing and extending the road to the venue. The show was attended by approximately 40,000 people and the city of Budva holds the distinction of being the smallest town ever to host a Rolling Stones gig.

From early 2009, the organizers began touting the Live Music Festival to be held during summer 2009 with acts such as Tina Turner, Britney Spears, and Zucchero being announced.

After a three-year absence, the musical performances returned in summer 2012 with the three-day event called Summer Fest organized from 5–8 August. Instead of globally known acts, the festival featured local ones such as: Nagual, Night Shift, Van Gogh, Hladno Pivo, Nipplepeople, Off Duty, S.A.R.S., Pero Defformero, Partibrejkers, Riblja Čorba, The Beatshakers, Gomila Nesklada, Who See, Prljavi Inspektor Blaža i Kljunovi, Kiki Lesendrić &

Piloti, Orthodox Celts, and Junior Jack.

Sea Dance Festival 2014, a three-day summer music festival, was held at Jaz beach from 15 to 17 July 2014. The festival, which was part of the EXIT Adventure, hosted "BE HUMAN!" charity event at the Dukley Gardens.

23. Mercur

Bus stations and top nosh are usually mutually exclusive territories, but this marvellous restaurant is the exception to the rule. For starters, it sits in a gorgeous green oasis populated by peacocks, deer and goats; there's also a playground. The menu is Montenegrin to the core, with superb grilled and baked *(ispod sač)* meats, spicy soups and local seafood. The prices are ridiculously low.

24. Archaeological Museum Budva

Archaeological Museum in Budva has a rich archaeological collection which began to form after the archaeological excavations conducted and at the end of the 50s of the last century. The exhibits showing about the rich cultural and historical heritage of the city, from the aboriginal inhabitants of the Illyrians, through the Greek, Roman, Slovenian culture tribes until recent history when in Budva or its surroundings have ,lived artisans, merchants, sailors, farmers, herders and fishermen, so long history of over 2500 years.

25. The Dancing Girl

Along the way we passed the gymnastic elegance of the statue of the Dancing Girl which stands by the water edge, albeit only on one leg.

It is a bit of a mystery as not much is known about the statue. One story relates that it was a tribute to the daughter of a rich family who drowned in the sea.

It is also considered to bring good luck if you rub certain erogenous parts of the structure.

This is obvious by the polished parts of the otherwise darkened statue.

This was the last chapter about Budva. Let’s go on and visit another city in the next chapters.

26. Kotor

Kotor (Montenegrin Cyrillic: Котор, pronounced [kɔ̌tɔr]; Italian: *Cattaro*) is a coastal town in Montenegro. It is located in a secluded part of the Gulf of Kotor. The city has a population of 13,510 and is the administrative center of Kotor Municipality.

The old Mediterranean port of Kotor is surrounded by fortifications built during the Venetian period. It is located on the Bay of Kotor (*Boka Kotorska*), one of the most indented parts of the Adriatic Sea. Some have called it the southern-most fjord in Europe, but it is a ria, a submerged river canyon. Together with the nearly overhanging limestone cliffs of Orjen and Lovćen, Kotor and its surrounding area form an impressive and picturesque Mediterranean landscape.

In recent years, Kotor has seen an increase in tourists, many of them coming by cruise ship. Visitors are attracted by the natural environment of the Gulf of Kotor and by the old town of Kotor. Kotor is part of the World Heritage Site dubbed the Natural and Culturo-Historical Region of Kotor. The fortified city of Kotor was also included in UNESCO's World Heritage Site list as part of Venetian Works of Defence between 15th and 17th centuries: *Stato da Terra* – western *Stato da Mar* in 2017.

27. Kotor Cathedral

The **Cathedral of Saint Tryphon** in Kotor is one of two Roman Catholic cathedrals in Montenegro. It is the seat of the Catholic Bishopric of Kotor which covers the entire gulf, currently led by Bishop Monsignor Ilija Janjić.

The cathedral was consecrated on 19 June 1166.[1] Compared to other buildings, the Kotor Cathedral is one of the largest and most ornate buildings in Kotor. The cathedral was seriously damaged and rebuilt after the 1667 Dubrovnik earthquake, but there were not enough funds for its complete reconstruction.

The April 1979 Montenegro earthquake, which completely devastated the Montenegro coast, also greatly damaged the cathedral. Luckily, it has been salvaged and the careful restoration of parts of its interior has not been completed until a few years ago. The Romanesque architecture, contains a rich collection of artifacts. Older than many famous churches and cathedrals in Europe, the cathedral has a treasury of immense value. In its interior there are frescoes from the 14th century, a stone ornament above the main altar in which the life of St Tryphon is depicted, as well as a relief of saints in gold and silver.

The collection of art objects includes a silver hand and a cross, decorated with ornaments and figures in relief. It is only a part of the valuable objects of the Treasury of this unique sacral building which was the City Hall in the past. Today, it is the best known tourist attraction in Kotor and a symbol of the city: the Saint is depicted in the city's coat of arms, along with a lion and the Mount of San Giovanni.

28. Our Lady Of The Rocks

Our Lady of the Rocks is one of the two islets off the coast of Perast in Bay of Kotor, Montenegro (the other being Sveti Đorđe Island). It is an artificial island created by bulwark of rocks and by sinking old and seized ships loaded with rocks. The Roman Catholic **Church of Our Lady of the Rocks**(Italian: *Chiesa della Madonna dello Scarpello*) is the largest building on the islet; it has a museum attached. There is also a small gift shop close to the church and a navigation light at the western end of the islet.

According to legend, the islet was made over the centuries by Croat local seamen who kept an ancient oath after finding the icon of Madonna and Child on the rock in the sea on July 22, 1452. Upon returning from each successful voyage, they laid a rock in the Bay. Over time, the islet gradually emerged from the sea. The custom of throwing rocks into the sea is alive even nowadays. Every year on the sunset of July 22, an event called *fašinada* in the local dialect, when local residents take their boats and throw rocks into the sea, widening the surface of the island, takes place.

Church was upgraded in 1722. The church contains 68 paintings by Tripo Kokolja, a famous 17th-century baroque artist from Perast. His most important painting, ten meters long, is *The Death of the Virgin*. There are also paintings by Italian artists, and an icon (circa 1452) of *Our Lady of the Rocks*, by Lovro Dobričević of Kotor. The church also houses a collection of silver votive tablets and a famous votive tapestry embroidered by Jacinta Kunić-Mijović from Perast. It took her 25 years to finish it while waiting for her darling to come from a long journey, and eventually, she became blind. She used golden and silver fibres but what makes this tapestry so famous is the fact that she also embroidered her own hair in it.

29. Grgurina Palace

Grgurina Palace is located on the square in Kotor, which occupies the central part of the urban core. Family Grgurina in the second half of the 17th century moved to Kotor from Koper (Istria).

Dealing with electronic commerce, Grgurina gained considerable wealth, and soon they were aggregated in Kotor patricians.

The palace was built in the very beginning of the 18th century by Conte Grgurina Marko. Building is a typical example of mature Baroque -symmetrical main facade, with an emphasis on the vertical axis, which is dominated by balconies, profiled portals and main entrance. It was built with beautifully carved stone cubes from Korcula. Brackets, baluster, molded of door and other elements are treated material brought from Korcula.

The interior layout, especially the first floor ("piano nobile"), is typical for the baroque palace in the Bay. Around the great grand salon in the center are arranged four rooms. Large stone terrace with a loggia and walled garden with horticulture supplemented the Baroque impression. The terrace is fitted with a family coat of arms - goat (Capra in Italian), the symbol of the city of Koper, in memory of family's background.

30. Cats Museum

The idea of setting up a cats' museum was conceived after the donation by Countess di Montereale Mantica of a huge collection of period images.

This material was added to the collections of the International Cats' Adoption Centre "Badoer" in Venice and has become very interesting and large and in the last 10 years has increased owing to further donations and targeted purchases.

He importance of the material and the large number of works has given the idea of setting up a museum where the works may be seen not only by visitors, who will certainly arrive, but also by a wider public who might wish to get to know us through internet.

The Museum, however, is not concerned only with cats, but, through the interest this animal universally arouses in people, aimes at making people feel and show greater respect towards nature, the animals and the environment continually threatened by man.

How can't love other animals and nature those who love cats?

To pass on love for animals is possible for everybody by means of a wider knowledge and knowledge is the first step towards respect.

As a seat for our Museum we chose Kotor in Montenegro, a city on the extreme part of Dalmatia for various reasons: its quietness, charming position and its situation of " ideal city for cats" as the population is fond of felines.

The Museum has activated the option in order to let all sympathizers know our works through the web. Actually a service is active by which a daily mail is sent to all those who ask for it, so that all can feel near to us and receive every day a different image from our collections.

We warmly thank in advance those who will send

further material to increase our collections or propose us to buy objects of their own.

"Lord Byron was right. The Montenegrin coastline really is the most beautiful encounter between land and sea."

- Tatler

31. Sveti Đorđe

Ostrvo Sveti Đorđe is one of the two islets off the coast of Perast in Bay of Kotor, Montenegro (the other being Gospa od Škrpjela). Unlike Gospa od Škrpjela, it is a natural island.

A small action took place during the Siege of Cattaro on 14 October 1813 when the French held island was captured by a British and Sicilian naval force.

The island contains Saint George Benedictine monastery from the 12th century and the old graveyard for the old nobility from Perast and further from the whole Bay of Kotor.

32. Lovćen National Park

Lovćen is a mountain and national park in southwestern Montenegro.

Mount Lovćen rises from the borders of the Adriatic basin, closing the long and twisting bays of Boka Kotorska and making the hinterland to the coastal town of Kotor. The mountain has two imposing peaks, *Štirovnik* (1,749 m) and *Jezerski vrh* (1,657 m).

The mountain slopes are rocky, with numerous fissures, pits and deep depressions giving its scenery a specific look. Lovćen stands on the border between two completely different natural wholes, the sea and the mainland, and so it is under the influence of both climates. The specific connection of the life conditions has caused the development of the different biological systems. There are 1,158 plant species on Lovćen, four of which are endemic.

National park

The national park encompasses the central and the highest part of the mountain massif and covers an area of 62.20 km^2. It was proclaimed a national park in 1952. Besides Lovćen's natural beauties, the rich historical, cultural and architectural heritage of the area are protected by the national park.

The area has numerous elements of national construction. The old houses and village *guvna* are authentic as well as the cottages in *katuns*, summer settlements of cattlebreeders.

A particular architectural relic worth mentioning is the road, winding uphill from Kotor to the village of Njeguši, the birthplace of Montenegro's royal family, the House of Petrović.

33. Have A Tipple Or Two

Montenegro has a lively nightlife, and thanks to the influx of backpackers and young travelers over the past few years, it's only growing faster. If you're so inclined to experience the Old Town of Kotor when the sun goes down, start out at the Wine Bar, a friendly little locale with some outdoor seating. Try some local wines, like Vranac or Pro Corde.

All the pubs and bars shut down at 1 a.m., but then you can make your way to Maximus, a massive and always busy nightclub just outside the city walls.

34. Maritime Museum of Montenegro

The Maritime Museum of Montenegro in Kotor has grown out of the collection founded by the "Boka Marine" Fraternity, around the year 1880 and opened to public in 1900. It gradually enlarged and in 1938, it was re-arranged and opened to visitors on the first floor of the present Museum building. It was only after the end of World War II, in the period 1949-1952, that the whole building, Baroque palace of the noble Grgurina family from the beginning of the 18th century, was completely restored and adaptet to meet the needs of the Museum.

The disastrous earthquake of April 15,1979, caused halt in regular activities of the Museum, its building being considerably damaged. In the period from 1982 to 1984, conservation and restoration works were finished and after the five year period of renovation, the Museum continued its activities.

35. Perast

One of the principal attractions on the Bay of Kotor is the ancient village of Perast, rich in Venice-like architecture which includes sixteen Baroque palaces, seventeen Catholic churches, several important Orthodox structures and a series of nine defensive towers, all set in stone and seemingly untouched by the scourge of modern-day tourism. Perast was a joyful stopping spot for the Russian Czars and Venetian Princes who for hundreds of years have frequented Kotor Bay to hone their sailing skills under the watchful gaze of abundant natural beauty, and today enjoys the worldly distinction as an important protected UNESCO world heritage site.

Those who are familiar with Perast's famous cousin to the north, Venice, will immediate recognize how the town has followed the Venetian tradition of building soaring churches on many of the small islands that overlook the town, including the Island of St. George where the 12th Century Benedictine monastery of St. George is located, and the neighboring island of Gospa od Skrpjela (Our Lady of the Rock). The abbey on the Island of St. George was reputedly built in the 9th Century and is a testament to Perast's rich architectural history, which is unparalleled in the region.

View of Perast from the slopes of Mt Orjen Matija Zmajevic (1680-1735) became admiral of the Russian Baltic fleet and was one of the main shipbuilders of the Russian Czar Peter the Great. He distinguished himself in many sea battles with the Swedes, for which he was awarded the Alexander Nevski medal.

There are many more famous men from Perast who immortalized the city not only for its beauty but also for the deeds and success of its inhabitants.

Among Montenegro's many treasures, the Bay of Kotor, including the town of Perast and the nearby islands of Our

Lady of the Rocks (Gospa od Skrpjela) and St. George provide the opportunity to take part in a rich history set among stunningly beautiful surroundings.

For some of these attractions we have talked before and you know the history and why you should visit them. This was the last chapter for the city of Kotor.

Let's go and see why other cities are worth visiting.

36. Ulcinj

Ulcinj is a town on the southern coast of Montenegro and the capital of Ulcinj Municipality. It has an urban population of 10,707 (2011), the majority being Albanians.

As one of the oldest settlements in the Adriatic coast, it was founded in 5th century BC. It was captured by the Romans in 163 BC from the Illyrians. With the division of the Roman Empire, it became part of the Byzantine Empire. During the Middle Ages it was under South Slavic rule for a few centuries. In 1405 it became part of Republic of Venice and in 1571 part of Ottoman Empire. Ulcinj was ceded to the Principality of Montenegro in 1878. It is a former medieval Catholic bishopric and remains a Latin titular see.

Ulcinj is a famous destination for tourists, because of its Long Beach, Lake Šas, Ada Bojana Island and for its two-millennia-old Ulcinj Castle. Ulcinj is also the centre of the Albanian community in Montenegro.

37. Long Beach

Velika Plaža is a beach in Ulcinj Municipality, Montenegro. It stretches from Port Milena in Ulcinj to Bojana River, which separates it from Ada Bojana.

Overview

The sand beach's length is 12,000 meters (8 miles), one of the longest in Europe and the longest beach in Montenegro.

The New York Times included Velika plaža and Montenegro's South Coast (including Ada Bojana and Hotel Mediteran in a ranking of top travel destinations for 2010 - "Top Places to Go in 2010".

Future Development

Velika plaža is natural asset of Montenegro that the government hopes to see developed as part of the country's tourism development strategy, albeit in an environmentally friendly manner. The vast hinterland of the beach is mostly undeveloped, so it is potentially the site of the biggest greenfield investment on Montenegrin coast.

So far, a public competition has been announced on creating a masterplan of developing a sustainable waterfront community, through means of public private partnership.

Kitesurfing spot

Velika plaza beach, near Ulcinj in Montenegro is the premier kiteboarding location on the Adriatic Coast. Fourteen kilometres strip of petty sand beach with strong cross onshore winds almost every day during summer afternoons makes it ideal for safe learning. Set in a protected natural area, surrounded by dunes and hidden by alluvial forests you will find the perfect spot to spend summer holidays on your own, with friends or your family.

It is hard to find better and safer surrounding to learn kiteboarding than here. Shallow, warm water and constant thermal wind make learning here a pure joy. No obstacles in or out of the water. Tides don't affect riding or safety.

Current is not that strong to present any significant danger. During the summer average temperature is 34°C, water temperature average is 23°C. Along the beach you can ride superb chop and wave conditions most of the time. Flat water spot is located at the southeast end of the beach, inside the river mouth.

There are a number of kitesurfing schools along the beach.

38. Lake Šas

Lake Šas is a lakelocated north-east of Ulcinj, near the village of Šas, in Montenegro. It is bordered geographically by Briska Gora (Mali i Brisë) to the southwest, Fraskanjelsko Polje (Këneta e Fraskanjellit) to the east, Ambulsko Brdo (Mali i Amullit) and Šasko Brdo (Mali i Shasit) to the northeast and the Brisko Polje (Fusha e Brisë) to the northwest. Geopolitically, Briska Gora lies to the southwest of Lake Šas, Fraskanjel lies to the east

and Ambula and Šas to the northeast. The area of this lake is 5.5 km², it is 3.2 km long and 1.5 km wide. The max depth is 7.8 m. The shore of the lake is about 8.6 km.

It is also known as *Little Lake Scutari*, because it has the same flora and fauna as Lake Scutari, which is much larger in size than Lake Šas. In warmer months, the lake is populated with large numbers of different bird species.

39. Ada Bojana

Ada Bojana is an island in the Ulcinj Municipality in Montenegro. The name *Ada* means river island in Serbian.

The island is created by a river delta of the Bojana River. Legend says it was formed by gathering river sand around a ship sunk at the mouth of Bojana river, but it is more likely to be a delta in formation. It is located on the southernmost tip of Montenegro, with only the Bojana river separating it from Pulaj and Velipojë in the Albanian territory.

The island is of triangular shape, bordered from two sides by the Bojana river, and by the Adriatic Sea from the south-west. It has an area of 4.8 square km.

It is a popular tourist destination, with 3 kilometres (2 miles) long sandy beach with traditional seafood restaurants. Ada Bojana is one of the premier kitesurfing and windsurfing locations on the Adriatic Coast with strong cross onshore winds during summer afternoons. Ada Bojana's main income is from Camping

The New York Times included Ada Bojana and Montenegro's South Coast (including Velika Plaža and Hotel Mediteran) in a ranking of top travel destinations for 2010 - "Top Places to Go in 2010".

40. Ulcinj Castle

Stari grad, **Kalaja** or **Ulcinj Castle** also known as **Ulcinj Old Town** is an ancient castle and neighborhood in Ulcinj, Montenegro. Today mostly inhabited by Albanians, it was built by the Illyrians and Ancient Greeks on a small peninsula at the right side of the Pristan Gulf, which is part of the Adriatic Sea. Today, oldest remains are the Cyclopean Wall. The castle has been restored many times since it was first built although major changes were made by the Byzantinians, Serbs, Venetians, and Ottomans. The modern city of Ulcinj was built outside of this castle.

Castle walls

Ulcinj's **Old Town** is one of the oldest urban architectural complexes on the Adriatic Sea. The castle, which some believe resembles a stranded ship, and the surrounding areas have flourished for about 25 centuries. Through the centuries, a variety of cultures and civilizations melded together. The Old Town represents a cultural and historical monument of invaluable significance due to its Illyrian walls, its citadel, the network of streets, the markets and town squares. It was built 2,500 years ago under economic, military, and cultural conditions quite different from those of today. The town's walls were often destroyed in wars, and just as quickly rebuilt by residents to keep their fortresses and residences safe. In doing so, they also preserved the beauty of this ancient town.

Old town has picturesque narrow and curved streets typical of the Middle Ages, densely packed two- and three-story stone houses decorated with elements of the Renaissance and Baroque, and finally a series of valuable edifices from the Ottoman time. The oldest remnants of the walls date back to the Illyrian period. In the 6th century, the town had two gates: the lower (eastern), which can be reached from the sea-side and the upper (western), which can be reached from land.

"When Pearls of Nature were sown, it was with a full hand that they were cast on this soil."

\- *Lord Byron*

41. Ladies Beach

Ladies Beach is a beach in Ulcinj, Montenegro. It is one of many beaches in Montenegro's South Coast with a special following among visitors to the region, as well as local residents.

Ladies Beach is known for its curious waters, a mixture of sulfur from an underwater spring, radium and sea salts. Pine resin from the sea trees at Ladies Beach, wafts in the air above the beach. Locals have long believed that Ladies Beach and its sea caves offer curative powers for ailments, and specific help to women with fertility issues.

Ulcinj Riviera has a predisposition for elite and health tourism, while “Ladies’ Beach” offer is definitely a peculiar one. In the shallows of “Ladies’ Beach” springs sulfur-mineral water. Thermal water is for the first time tested 81 years ago, when its effective action was pointed. “Ladies’ Beach” has an effective action, not only for gynecological diseases, primary and secondary infertility, but also for diseases of respiratory and of the digestive tract. The sulfuric beach is located in a bay, in the middle of pine forest, presenting an ideal setting for the treatment of above mentioned diseases by natural factors. Sulfuric water springs in the shallows. When waves splash clean sulfuric seawater, they create ideal micro and macro molecules suitable for natural aerosol therapy.

42. Museum Of Local History

Museum of Local History in Ulcinj or simply **Museum of Ulcinj** is a local museum located in Kalaja, part of Ulcinj, Montenegro.

Through exhibits from the archaeological, ethnographic and artistic collection, in the Museum of Local History you can learn about life in Ulcinj from the 5th century BC to the Turkish period.

The Museum is located in the Church-Mosque, which was built as a church in 1510, and had been transformed to a mosque by the Turks in 1571. Within the archaeological collection, there is an exhibition of antique Greek and Roman ceramics, glass, coins as well as items which show the time of the sovereignty of the Montenegrin dynasties of Vojislavljević and Balšić. In the part of the exhibition that displays items from the ethnographic collection, there are traditional costumes, mostly Albanian, jewelry and local handcraft which show the variety of folklore creativity in this area.

The museum is divided into:

- Archaeological Museum (in the Church-Mosque building)
- Ethnological Museum
- Art Gallery (in the Tower of the Balšić)
- Other archaeological exhibits (in the cells surrounding the slave market)

43. Go Kite Surfing

Dolcinium is the first established Montenegrin kite club, which successfully left behind nine years of satisfied clients and friends. It is the best place you could imagine to learn how to kite or progress your current level.

When you come to Dolcinium, a warm, soft & loving environment will be waiting for you. Relaxing beach beds, friendly and professional service make it a wonderful all-day destination. Flying kites all over the horizon, delicious and fresh Mediterranean food, relaxed atmosphere, good vibes and good music are a must at Dolcinium.

Dolcinium won the Wild Beauty Award in 2011, as the most attractive offer in Montenegro.

Come and enjoy at Dolcinium the taste of the sea, sun, sand and kitesurfing. Sandy feet and friendly faces, chill-out music, refreshing cocktails and yellow sunsets, you can have it all!

44. Mother Theresa Statue

Aptly located at Ulcinj's medical clinic is a statue of Mother Theresa, the most famous Albanian of recent years (although she was actually born in Macedonia). The statue receives dozen of floral bouquets daily.

Adjacent to it is a commemorative plaque reading 'In gratitude to the people of Ulcinj for the humanity, solidarity and hospitality they have shown in sheltering and taking care of the persecuted from Kosova during the period March '98 to June '99 – Grateful Kosovars'.

45. St Nicholas' Cathedral

Set among a picturesque grove of gnarled olive trees just below the Upper Gate is this Orthodox cathedral. It's a relative newbie, having been built in 1890 shortly after the Ottomans were booted out, although it's believed to stand on the site of a 15th-century monastery.

This was the last chapter about Ulcinj. After including the most interesting activities, beaches and sightseeing in the main Montenegrin cities, we're going to talk about what to do in the small, not so well known, cities.

46. Bar Cycling Tour

Cycle though villages where olive harvesting were major agricultural occupation of locals. Pass on of the oldest olive tree in the World. When you finish a ride visit Old town of Bar one of the largest and the most important medieval archaeological site in the Balkans.

After your guide meets you at Marina in Port of Bar you will be transferred to the old road which once connected Old town of Ulcinj with Old town of Bar. After short instruction, paddle with your guide through Mediterranean villages towards Old town of Bar (Stari Bar). Before this was the only road that locals used when selling their local products such as olives, olive oil, citrus fruits, goat cheese on green market in Stari Bar. Beside local villages your view will be occupied with stunning panoramas at riviera from Utjeha to Bar. Stop at Stara maslina - one of the world's oldest olive trees located near Stari Bar. It is said to be over 2,000 years old. When you finish a ride you will have time to visit remains of the old town of Stari Bar ('Old Bar'). Over the centuries it was taken over by the Venetians, the Austro-Hungarians and the Ottoman Empire. The residential architecture of the town is characterized by Late Gothic, Renaissance, Baroque and oriental elements. In 1979 Old Bar was destroyed by earthquake and its reconstruction was not completed. After visiting Old town of Bar return transfer to Marina of Port of Bar.

47. Cetinje

Sleepy **Cetinje** sits just over the mountainous crest from Budva and Kotor, and is well placed for a visit if you're heading between coast and interior. Cetinje became Montenegro's **capital** on independence in 1878, and of the clutch of embassies that were established, many remain visible today as faded relics of the city's proud past.

Though the status of capital has long been passed to Podgorica, many government offices – and, in fact, the presidential seat – remain in Cetinje. The town centre is small enough to walk around in an hour or two, and almost all sights are located on or near **Njegoševa**, a mostly pedestrianized central thoroughfare. Buses pull into a tiny terminal next to the *Sport* hotel. From here it's a 10min walk into town. Note that there's no tourist office in Cetinje.

48. Lake Skadar

Oozing over the Albanian border, beautiful **Skadar** is the largest lake in the Balkans, and also one of its most untouched. However, since it lies on the train line, it's easily accessible and can make a good stop off on your way to or from the coast. The main jump-off point is **Virpazar**, a cute little fishing village at the northern end of the lake, a kilometer back down the line to Podgorica from the station.

From here it's a pleasant walk along the lake's western shore, and though there's nowhere to rent bikes, if you've brought one along you'll be in heaven – an hour's ride will bring into sight a clutch of **offshore monasteries**, though to get any nearer you'll have to search for a boat.

Accommodation is available in Virpazar at the *Pelikan* which also has an excellent restaurant.

49. Herceg Novi

Developed as a coastal resort during eighteenth-century Austro-Hungarian rule, little **Herceg Novi** is a thoroughly likeable town, and yet one usually bypassed by tourists. Its steep maze of lanes is lined with stately, crumbling villas, while decades of international sailors have left a legacy of plants and flowers from around the world.

Most sights are concentrated within Herceg Novi's appealing, walled **Old Town**.

At its centre you'll find the **Church of Archangel Michael**, just over a hundred years old but looking a few decades more than that. From here you can climb the steps to take in views from the "bloody tower" of **Kanli Kula**. Downhill, the seafront **promenade** makes for a delightful walk. Head east for twenty minutes, then turn inland to find the elegant, seventeenth-century **Savina Monastery**.

50. Tivat

Tivat is a town full of changes and incredible destiny. It used to be the seaside resort for the rulers, nobility and poets in the Middle Ages. It enjoyed a peaceful history until the end of the 19th century. But than an Austrian admiral knocked on the door of Mayor of Tivat, captain Marko Krstovic, and announced the establishment of an Austro-Hungarian navy base on the Tivat bay coastline, and Tivat was a navy arsenal, a port and a dry dock. For over a century hundreds of handymen, turners, locksmiths and boat builders were trained in Tivat.

Tivat doesn't really have a center. When you come into the town, you should rather ask for Pine, the waterside promenade. Here you can enjoy the walk along the sea or have coffee and cakes in several café bars situated next to each other.

Tivat lacks sand or pebble beaches – instead they are of

the concrete-platform variety. There are, however, some lovely sandy beaches outside of town and on the Luštica peninsula. The city park, founded on the estate of Kotor noblemen in 1892, is a true botanical garden, an expansive area of fir, cedar and pine trees, as well as a range of exotic plants brought here by seafarers from all over the world.

> TOURIST

GREATER THAN A TOURIST

Visit GreaterThanATourist.com
http://GreaterThanATourist.com

Sign up for the Greater Than a Tourist Newsletter
http://eepurl.com/cxspyf

Follow us on Facebook:
https://www.facebook.com/GreaterThanATourist

Follow us on Pinterest:
http://pinterest.com/GreaterThanATourist

Follow us on Instagram:
http://Instagram.com/GreaterThanATourist

> TOURIST

GREATER THAN A TOURIST

Please leave your honest review of this book on Amazon and Goodreads. Thank you.

We appreciate your positive and negative feedback as we try to provide tourist guidance in their next trip from a local.

Our Story

Traveling is a passion of the "Greater than a Tourist" series creator. Lisa studied abroad in college, and for their honeymoon Lisa and her husband toured Europe. During her travels to Malta, an older man tried to give her some advice based on his own experience living on the island since he was a young boy. She was not sure if she should talk to the stranger but was interested in his advice. When traveling to some places she was wary to talk to locals because she was afraid that they weren't being genuine. Through her travels, Lisa learned how much locals had to share with tourists. Lisa created the "Greater Than a Tourist" book series to help connect people with locals. A topic that locals are very passionate about sharing.

Notes

Made in the USA
Middletown, DE
27 January 2023